Butcher's Hook:
Look

The Little Book of
COCKNEY
RHYMING SLANG

JOHN LAWRENCE

RUNNING PRESS
PHILADELPHIA · LONDON

A Running Press Miniature Edition™
Copyright © 1995 by John Lawrence.
Printed in Singapore
All rights reserved under the Pan-American and
International Copyright Conventions.

British Library Cataloguing-in-Publication Data. A
catalogue record for this book is available from the
British Library.
ISBN 1–56138–422–4
This book may be ordered by mail from the publisher.
Please include £1.00 for postage and handling.
But try your bookstore first!
Running Press Book Publishers
Cedar House
35 Chichele Road
Oxted, Surrey RH8 0AE

for
Myra

About this book

Rhyming slang first came to light in early Victorian England as a secret language used by thieves to hoodwink the law and outwit authority. It probably did not originate in the underworld, however, but among the numerous gangs of Irish and Cockney workmen who made up a large percentage of the force employed in building the railways and other massive construction works of the time. From there it spread to the underworld, and was later taken up by other sections of society. It particularly flourished in London's East End, hence its accepted name of 'Cockney Rhyming Slang'.

It travelled to Australia and also to the United States, where it is known as 'Australian Slang'. The authority on the subject is Julian Franklyn's *Dictionary of Rhyming Slang*.

This unique language with its famous phrases ('trouble and strife'—'wife', 'bees and honey'—'money', 'plates of meat'—'feet' are three of the best known) is still in use in different versions, and many people use it without being aware of doing so. Very often the rhyme part of the phrase is dropped, which leads to much confusion for the uninitiated (a good example is that then 'plates' stands for 'feet').

The set of illustrations in this book is based on a loose sequence of rhymes. The pictures grew out of an association of words and there is the thread of a story if you care to find it. I leave you to use your 'mincers' and take a 'butcher's' at the following pages.

—John Lawrence

Apples & Pears : Stairs

Cat & Mouse : House

Noah's Ark : Park

Brown Hat : Cat

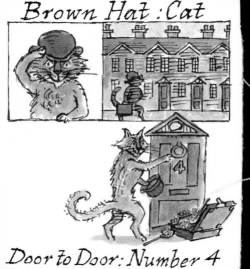

Door to Door: Number 4

Trouble & Strife :
Wife

China Plate:

Chopsticks:

Mate

Six

Bended Knees:

Cheese

Brothers & Sisters.

Gay & Frisky:

Whiskers

Whisky

Dickory Dock:

Clock

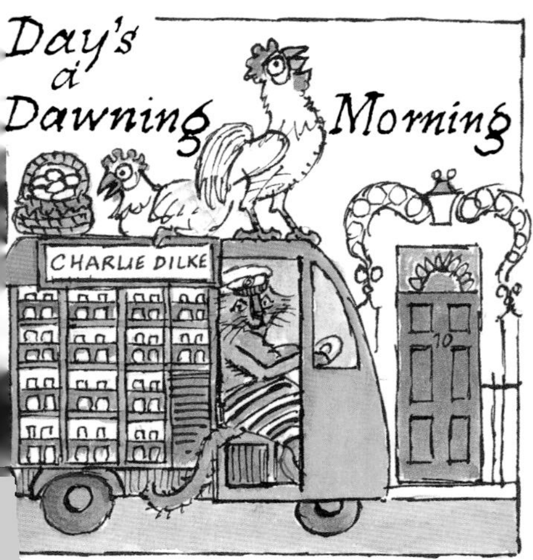

Cock & Hen :Number 10

Borrow & Beg

Rank & Riches: Breeche,

rog & Toad : Road

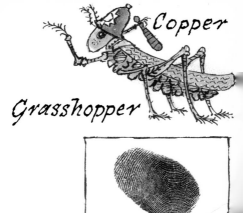

Copper

Grasshopper

Inky Smudge

Es : Money

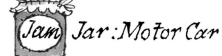

Jam Jar : Motor Car

Rolls Royce: Voice

Joe Hook : Crook

Judge

Flowery Dell: Cell

Sighs & Tears: Ear

Mince Pies:

Eyes

Jam Tarts:

Sweethearts

Heavenly Bliss

Kiss

Ship in full Sail:

Pint of Ale

Cape
of
Good
Hope

These & Those : Toe

Botany Bay:
Run Away

Kick & Prance: Danc

Plates of Meat:Feet

April Showers

Flowers

Barnet Fair : Hair

Lion's Lair : Chair

Rose Lea

Charles James
Fox : Box

Soup & Gravy:

Navy

All Afloat: Coat

Rolling Billows:

Pillows

ABOUT THE ARTIST

John Lawrence has illustrated more
than one hundred books for children
and adults. A fellow of the Royal
Society of Printmakers and the Society
of Wood Engravers, his work is in the
collections of the Victoria and Albert
Museum, and the Ashmolean Museum
in Oxford. He lives with his family
in London.

This book has been bound using handcraft methods,
and Smyth-sewn to ensure durability.

The dust jacket was designed by Toby Schmidt.

The interior was illustrated and designed, and the
text was compiled by John Lawrence.

The text was set in Berkeley Book and Greco Deco.

Jackdaw & Rook:
Book

Bo-Peep : Sleep